# THE WEAPONS ENCYCLOPÆDIA
## TANK  AIRCRAFT  AFV  SHIP  ARTILLERY  VEHICLES  SECRET WEAPON

TWE-028 ENG

BRITISH TANK CRUSADER

# THE WEAPONS ENCYCLOPAEDIA

## EDITORIAL STAFF
Luca Stefano Cristini, Paolo Crippa.

## ACADEMIC STAFF
Enrico Acerbi, Massimiliano Afiero, Aldo Antonicelli, Ruggero Calò, Luigi Carretta, Flavio Chistè, Anna Cristini, Carlo Cucut, Salvo Fagone, Enrico Finazzer, Arturo Giusti, Björn Huber, Andrea Lombardi, Aymeric Lopez, Marco Lucchetti, Gabriele Malavoglia, Luigi Manes, Giovanni Maressi, Francesco Mattesini, Daniele Notaro, Péter Mujzer, Federico Peirani, Alberto Peruffo, Maurizio Raggi, Andrea Alberto Tallillo, Antonio Tallillo, Roberto Vela, Massimo Zorza.

## PUBLISHED BY
Luca Cristini Editore (Soldiershop), via Orio, 35/4 - 24050 Zanica (BG) ITALY.

## DISTRIBUTION BY
Soldiershop - www.soldiershop.com, Amazon, Ingram Spark, Berliner Zinnfigurem (D), LaFeltrinelli, Mondadori, Libera Editorial (Spain), Google book (eBook), Kobo, (eBoook), Apple Book (eBook).

## PUBLISHING'S NOTES
None of unpublished images or text of our book may be reproduced in any format without the expressed written permission of Luca Cristini Editore (already Soldiershop.com) when not indicate as marked with license creative commons 3.0 or 4.0. Luca Cristini Editore has made every reasonable effort to locate, contact and acknowledge rights holders and to correctly apply terms and conditions to Content. Every effort has been made to trace the copyright of all the photographs. If there are unintentional omissions, please contact the publisher in writing at: info@soldiershop.com, who will correct all subsequent editions.

## LICENSES COMMONS
This book may utilize part of material marked with license creative commons 3.0 or 4.0 (CC BY 4.0), (CC BY-ND 4.0), (CC BY-SA 4.0) or (CC0 1.0). We give appropriate attribution credit and indicate if change were made in the acknowledgments field. Our WTW books series utilize only fonts licensed under the SIL Open Font License or other free use license.

## CONTRIBUTORS OF THIS VOLUME & ACKNOWLEDGEMENTS
We would like to thank the main contributors to this issue: The profiles of the floats are all by the author. The colouring of the photos is by Anna Cristini. Special thanks to national and/or private institutions such as: Army General Staff, State Archives, Bundesarchiv, Nara, Library of Congress, Wikipedia, USAF, Signal magazine, War Chronicles, War Front, IWM, Australian War Museum, etc. A P.Crippa, A.Lopez, Péter Mujzer, L.Manes, C.Cucut, Tallillo archives. Model Victoria (www.modelvictoria.it) etc. for providing images or other items from their archives.

For a complete list of Soldiershop titles, or for every information please contact us on our website: www.soldiershop.com or www.cristinieditore.com. E-mail: info@soldiershop.com. Keep up to date on Facebook https://www.facebook.com/soldiershop.publishing

Title: BRITISH TANK CRUSADER  Code.: TWE-028 EN
Series by Luca Stefano Cristini
ISBN code: 9791255891475.  First edition July 2023
**THE WEAPONS ENCYCLOPAEDIA (SOLDIERSHOP)** is a trademark of Luca Cristini Editore

# THE WEAPONS ENCYCLOPÆDIA
TANK AIRCRAFT AFV SHIP ARTILLERY VEHICLES SECRET WEAPON

# BRITISH TANK CRUSADER

LUCA STEFANO CRISTINI

BOOK SERIES FOR MODELERS & COLLECTORS

# CONTENTS

**Introduction** ............................................................................................................. 5
- Development and project ................................................................................... 5
- Technical features ............................................................................................... 9
- Performances ..................................................................................................... 11

**Operational use** ........................................................................................................ 23
- Operation Battleaxe ............................................................................................ 23
- Operation Crusader ............................................................................................ 26
- Operation Bertram .............................................................................................. 26
- In Tunisia ............................................................................................................. 29

**Camouflage and distinctive signs** ........................................................................... 41
- European and metropolitan theatre colours .................................................... 41
- Middle Eastern and African theatre colours .................................................... 42
- Eastern colours ................................................................................................... 42

**Versions of the vehicle** ............................................................................................. 47

**Data sheet** .................................................................................................................. 52

**Bibliography** .............................................................................................................. 58

▼ A Crusader Mk. I with the small additional machine gun turret under construction, 1941.

# INTRODUCTION

The Crusader was one of the most significant British tanks of the Second World War; despite its low, aggressive silhouette, it was often outclassed as a combat tank, but remained in service until the end of the war in its various special versions. Over 5,000 units were built, contributing significantly to British victories in the North African campaign. Although the Crusader was not used outside Africa, its chassis was modified to create several variants, including anti-aircraft, fire support, observation, communication, bulldozer and recovery vehicles.

## ■ DEVELOPMENT AND PROJECT

The Mk VI cruiser tank, known as the Crusader, was developed almost at the same time as the Covenanter, but was a Nuffield design, equipped with the Nuffield Liberty Mk III engine and a Nuffield gearbox. Although the Crusader resembled the Covenanter in general appearance, it had several differences, including the number of load-bearing wheels: five on each side in the Crusader and four in the Covenanter. The Cruiser tank series began in 1936, when Vickers presented the War Office with a new, economical, medium-sized tank equipped with a commercial petrol engine, the A9E1. This model was considered a temporary solution pending production of the Christie suspension.

The prototype, designated as the A15, had an unusual feature: two small turrets at the front, one for the pilot and the other, opposite him, for a machine gunner. Both turrets were equipped with a 7.92 mm machine gun, but after initial trials, both the gun and the pilot's turret were removed. The tests also revealed engine cooling problems and defects in the gearbox. These and other problems took a long time to resolve and many remained unresolved when the tank ended its career.

▲ Crusader Mk. I preserved in the Tank Museum of the Royal Australian Armoured Corps.

The first Crusader Mark I tanks entered service in 1941 and, despite their agility, were characterised by light armour and insufficient armament. Armed with a 40 mm cannon and 40 mm basic armour, it was already outdated by the time it entered service and, as there were not enough 57 mm cannons available, only the armour thickness was increased to 50 mm, resulting in the Crusader II.

The later Crusader Mark II had a maximum armour of 49 mm (1.9 inches) and the main armament of the Crusader Mark I and II was a 2-pound (40 mm) Ordnance QF gun.

A 57 mm cannon was finally installed on the Crusader III, at the expense of a crew member in the turret. This variant was able to adequately deal with the German Panzer III and Panzer IV medium tanks encountered in combat. Within the 1st Armoured Brigade, the Crusader proved crucial during the Second Battle of El Alamein, the siege of Tobruk and the Tunisian campaign, before being replaced by the US M4 Sherman.

In action, the Crusader proved fast and manoeuvrable, but its armour was consistently too thin; Crusaders armed with the 40 mm gun were no match for the equivalent German tanks. Poor reliability did not improve the chances of survival in the desert, but gradual improvements were made, and a 76.2 mm howitzer was fitted to the Crusader IICS.

Due to delays with its replacement, the Crusader remained in service until the end of 1942, when it was gradually replaced by US-supplied M3 Grant tanks and later by the aforementioned M4 Sherman. These changes were necessary due to the Crusader's reliability problems in the harsh desert conditions and the appearance of better-armoured and better-armoured German tanks in the Afrika Korps. Despite this, the Crusader was used in combat until the end of the war in North Africa and later for training in Britain.

▲ The same Crusader Mk. I in the Royal Australian Armoured Corps Tank Museum from another angle.

## CRUSADER MK. I, NORTH AFRICA 1941

▲ Crusader Mk. I in North Africa in the typical first three-colour camouflage.

▲ British Army soldiers examine an Arv version Crusader equipped with a front crane and armed with two Bren anti-aircraft guns.

Once retired as battle tanks, the Crusaders were used in various special versions. These included an anti-aircraft version armed with a 40 mm Bofors gun (Crusader III AA I) or with twin or triple 20 mm guns (Crusader III AA II). There was also a tank recovery version, the Crusader ARV, without a turret but equipped with an A-shaped boom crane. Another version, also without a turret, was equipped with a dozer shovel and served as an engineer's tank (Crusader Dozer). Many Crusaders were converted into high-speed artillery tractors (Crusader Gun Tractor) with an open body structure, which were used extensively in Europe in 1944 and 1945 for towing 76.2 mm (17 lb) anti-tank guns. Others were used for various experiments, such as the installation of new engines, demining devices and fording trials that led to the development of the Duplex Drive tanks.

## TECHNICAL FEATURES

Unlike the previous Christie cruisers (the A13 Mk III and Mk IV tanks and the Mk V Covenanter), which had four load-bearing wheels, the Crusader had five on each side to improve weight distribution, in a tank that weighed almost 20 tonnes compared to the 14 tonnes of the previous cruisers. The **wheels**, 32 inches (810 mm) in diameter, were made of pressed steel with solid rubber tyres. The sides of the **hull** consisted of two separate plates, with the suspension arms between them.

The Crusader had a different **engine** from the Covenanter, a different steering system and a conventional cooling system with radiators in the engine compartment. While the Covenanter used a newly designed engine, the Crusader adapted the already available Liberty engine to fit into a lower engine compartment. On the port side of the front of the hull, where the engine radiator was located in the Covenanter, was a small hand-operated auxiliary turret armed with a Besa machine gun. This auxiliary turret was awkward to operate and was often removed in the field or left unused.

Both the A13 Mk III Covenanter and A15 Crusader used the same main **turret.** This was polygonal, with the sides widening and then narrowing again, to maximise space on the limited diameter of the turret ring. The first production vehicles had a cast 'semi-internal' **gun** shroud, which was quickly replaced in production by a larger, better-protected shroud with three vertical slots for the main gun, a coaxial Besa machine gun and the sighting telescope. There was no commander's cupola, which instead had a flat hatch with the periscope mounted through it.

▲ Crusader AA Mk. II. This is the anti-aircraft version armed with two twin 20mm machine guns.

## CRUSADER MK. I 7TH ARMOURED DIVISION

▲ Crusader Mk. I belonging to the 7th Armoured Division, 22nd Armoured Brigade. North African Front, 1942.

The main **armament**, as in other British tanks of the time, was balanced so that the gunner could control its elevation through a padded rod against the right shoulder, rather than using a gear mechanism. This fitted well with the British doctrine of firing accurately on the move.

When it became clear that there would be delays in the introduction of the next heavy cruisers (Cavalier, Centaur and Cromwell), the Crusader was adapted with a six-pounder gun.

## PERFORMANCES

The initial performance of the Crusader was superior to that of the Stuart light tanks. Although the Crusader had reliability problems, it became the main tank for British armoured regiments, while the Stuarts were used for reconnaissance.

In North Africa, the Crusader faced chronic reliability problems due to several factors: the tanks that arrived often lacked the necessary tools and maintenance manuals, which were often stolen or lost during transport. The lack of spare parts meant that damaged parts were replaced with components salvaged from other damaged tanks. In maintenance depots, tanks were often repaired with components that were already at the limit of their service life.

The rapid increase in production in the UK led to quality problems, as inexperienced workers began to assemble the tanks, increasing the workload on maintenance depots that had to make corrections.

The new tanks also had design flaws. The reconfiguration of the Liberty Mk. III in a flatter format to fit the Crusader's engine compartment adversely affected the water pumps and cooling fans, which were critical in desert temperatures. Various modifications, official and unofficial, were applied to improve reliability and conserve the water needed to keep the vehicles operational. However, solving these problems took a long time and confidence in the Crusader declined. There were calls to replace the vehicles with Valentine tanks or American-made M3 Grants.

▲ A Crusader tank is loaded onto a special Scammell trailer ready to be returned to the forward areas after receiving repair work in a workshop in the rear. North Africa, 10 December 1941.

## CRUSADER MK. I CS (CLOSE-SUPPORT)

▲ Crusader Mk. I the partial absence of the mudguard allows the shape of the wagon to be seen in the track area.

▲ King George VI of the United Kingdom inspects a deployment of Crusader tank crews of the 26th Armoured Brigade in Scotland on 15 October 1942.

## CRUSADER MK. II OF THE 7TH ARMOURED DIVISION

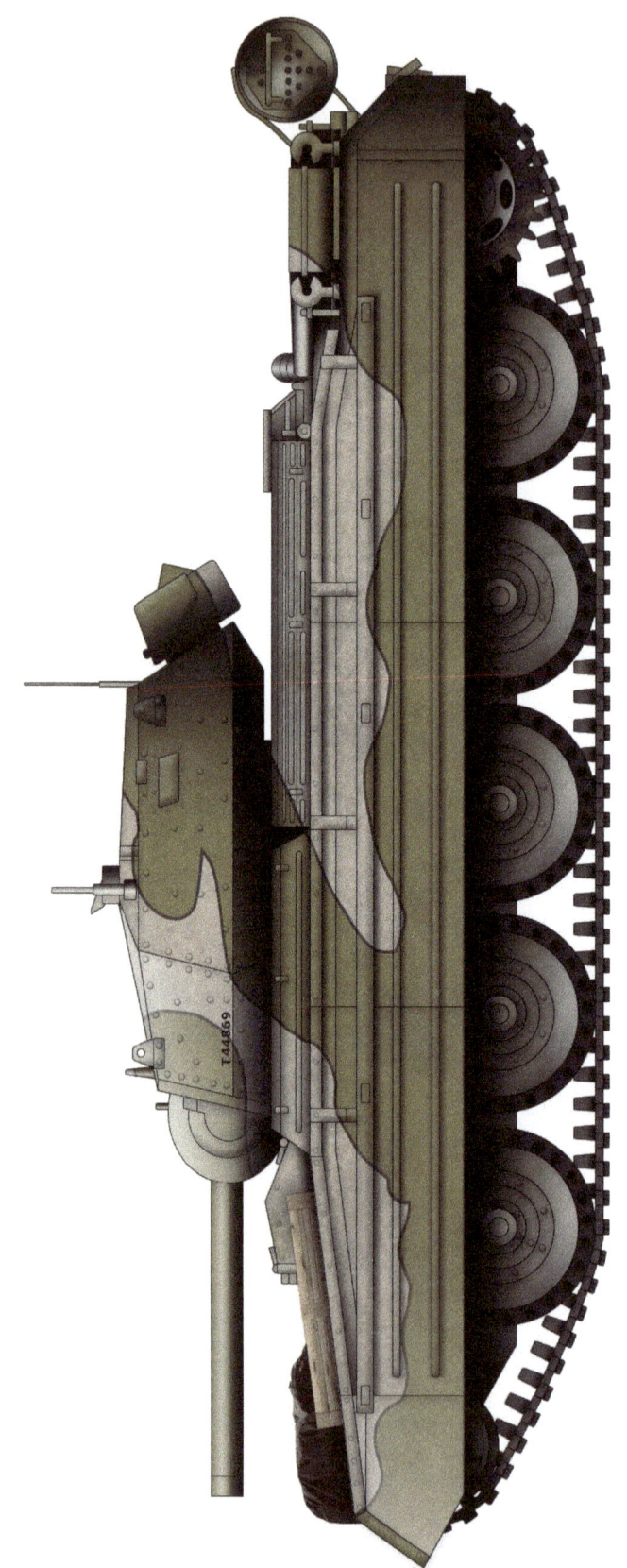

▲ Crusader Mk. II belonging to the 7th Armoured Division.

As time passed, more and more tanks were sent to maintenance depots, causing a shortage of combat-ready tanks and a huge backlog of repairs. The number of vehicles available on the front line decreased and US-made tanks were used.

The 2-pounder cannon had good initial performance, but ammunition supply was focused on armour-piercing (AP) shells. When the German tanks adopted hardened armour, no effective APCBC ammunition was available. When it finally became available, German tanks had already adapted to counter it. Delays in the production of the new generation of cruiser tanks led the Crusader to be armed with the 6-pounder gun, which offered significantly better anti-tank performance.

The Crusader, being a highly mobile cruiser tank, had lighter armour than Axis tanks. It was among the first to be fitted with additional armour for ammunition storage, greatly improving the vehicle's survivability with a slight reduction in the number of shells it could carry. However, the driver's compartment presented a significant vulnerability, with the side exposed after the removal of the secondary Besa machine gun turret, becoming a bullet trap.

Despite its many problems, the Crusader was successful in combat against Axis tanks, exploiting its superior mobility and ability to fire on the move to hit enemy vehicles' weak points. This caused the Germans to change tactics, simulating retreats to draw the Crusader towards a line of pre-positioned anti-tank guns. Without high-explosive (HE) ammunition, the Crusader struggled to engage these enemies. This situation persisted until the introduction of US vehicles, such as the Grant and Sherman, with 75mm dual-purpose guns.

▲ Crusader Mk. III armed with the powerful L 43 cannon. North African theatre, 1943.

▲ Cleaning of the 6-pdr gun barrel of a Crusader by its crew of the 16th/5th Lancers, 6th Armored Division. El Aroussa, Tunisia, May 1943.

▲ The Crusader found its main use mainly in the North African sector. Above is a Crusader Mk. II. Below, a Crusader II tank in the Western Desert, 2 October 1942.

## CRUSADER MK. II OF THE 7TH ARMOURED DIVISION

▲ Crusader Mk. II belonging to the 7th Armoured Division, Junior Battalion A Regiment (blue triangle).

▲ Tank Crusader Mk. III, on reconnaissance. 1 January 1943, North Africa.

Summary table of Crusader models produced during the conflict:

| Models | 1940 | 1941 | 1942 | 1943 | 1944 | 1945 | Total |
|---|---|---|---|---|---|---|---|
| Crusader Mk I | 2 | 248 | 0 | 0 | 0 | 0 | 250 |
| Crusader Mk II | 0 | 407 | 1405 | 0 | 0 | 0 | 1812 |
| Crusader Mk III | 0 | 0 | 946 | 771 | 0 | 0 | 1717 |
| Crusader AA Oerlikon | 0 | 0 | 91 | 345 | 299 | 0 | 735 |
| Crusader AA Bofors | 0 | 0 | 0 | 238 | 0 | 0 | 238 |
| Crusader OP | 0 | 0 | 0 | 112 | 0 | 0 | 112 |
| Crusader Tractor | 0 | 0 | 0 | 0 | 474 | 126 | 600 |
| Totals | 2 | 655 | 2442 | 1466 | 773 | 126 | 5464 |

# CRUSADER MK. II, "THE SAINT"

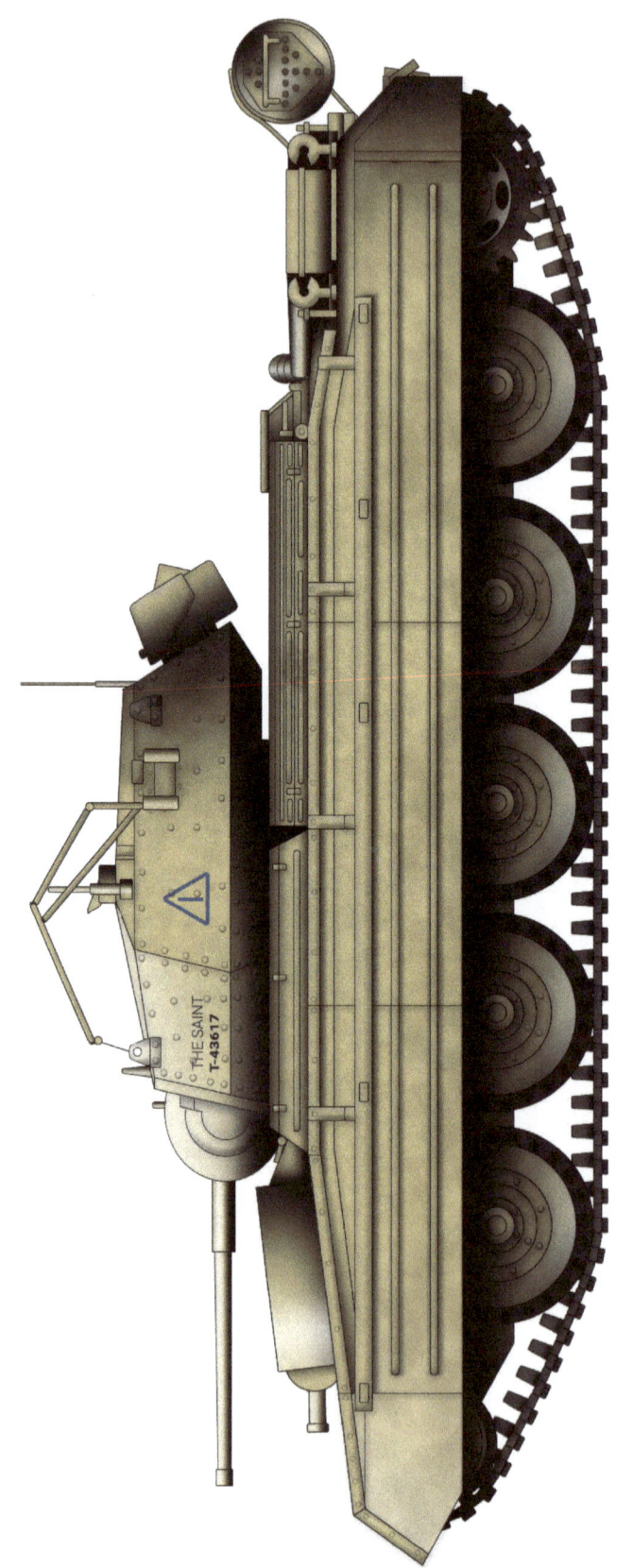

▲ Crusader Mk. II, 'The Saint', A Squadron, 10th Royal Hussars, 2nd Armoured Brigade, 1st Armoured Div.

▲ Crusader III tank equipped with sand guards. Note the pilot facing the front of the turret.

▼ The Crusader Mk. III at the head of a Sherman II armoured column makes its entrance at Mersa Matruh, Battle of El Alamein, November 1942.

▲ Some Crusader III tanks boarding a floating dock from a 'Spud' pontoon during testing of an artificial harbour, UK, 23 June 1943 (one year before D-Day).

# OPERATIONAL USE

The Crusader participated exclusively in military operations in North Africa. By early 1941, British forces in the region faced severe tank shortages, with only a few obsolete light tanks and cruisers to counter the more modern Panzer III and Panzer IV used by the Afrika Korps divisions.

To deal with this difficult situation, President Churchill urgently ordered a convoy of new tanks to be sent to Egypt. This order materialised in Operation Tiger, which brought 238 tanks ashore in Alexandria on 12 May 1941.

Their first action took place during 'Operation Battleaxe'. After the conclusion of this campaign, better tanks such as the Sherman and Cromwell became available, and the Crusaders were used for secondary tasks for the rest of the war: as a base for anti-aircraft installations or as artillery tractors. As anti-aircraft, they were designed for use in north-west Europe, but were not needed due to Allied air dominance. As artillery tractors, they were used in the regiments equipped with 17-pounder guns within the armoured divisions and with XII Army Corps.

## OPERATION BATTLEAXE

Operation Battleaxe (15-17 June 1941) was an offensive by the British Army to lift the siege of Tobruch and retake eastern Cyrenaica from German and Italian forces. It was the first time during the war that a significant German force fought on the defensive. The British lost more than half their tanks on the first day and only one of three attacks was successful.

▲ Crusader tanks moving towards advanced positions in the Western Desert, 26 November 1941.

## A15 CRUSADER MK. II

▲ A15 Crusader Mk. II (QF 2 pdr, 40 mm cannon).

On the second day, the British had mixed results, retreating on their western flank and repelling a large German counterattack in the centre. On the third day, the British narrowly avoided disaster by retreating just before a German encirclement movement. Battleaxe's failure led to the replacement of British General Sir Archibald Wavell, Commander-in-Chief of the Middle East, by Claude Auchinleck; Wavell assumed Auchinleck's position as Commander-in-Chief of India.

The Axis forces, pushing the British troops as far as the Egyptian border with a mixture of older tanks and a few remaining Matilda infantry tanks, were quickly resupplied by sea across the Mediterranean, arriving, as mentioned above, on 12 May 1941. A sufficient number of Crusaders were destined for the equipment of the 6th Royal Tank Regiment, which together with the older cruiser tanks of the 2nd Royal Tank Regiment formed the 7th Armoured Brigade. The other tanks were Matilda Infantry tanks assigned to 4th Armoured Brigade, bringing 7th Armoured Division to deploy only four armoured regiments.

Despite pressure from London to bring 7th Armoured Division into action, the time taken to prepare the Crusaders for the desert and train them delayed their first deployment until Operation Battleaxe, an attempt to break the siege of Tobruch the following June. During the brigade's advance along the enemy flank, the Crusaders were surprised by hidden anti-tank guns and lost eleven tanks. Over the next two days, the 6RTR suffered further losses from enemy actions and failures to retreat fighting.

The 7th Armoured Brigade was then re-equipped with new Crusaders, but, due to the expansion of the brigade with the addition of the 7th Hussars, not enough Crusaders were available to replace all the old cruisers.

▲ Crusader tank captured by Axis forces and now in German service, Afrika Korps, 1942.

To increase the strength of the 7th Armoured Division to three armoured brigades, the 22nd Armoured Brigade, consisting of three inexperienced armoured regiments equipped with Crusader, was transferred to North Africa. The 8th Hussars were added to the 4th Armoured Brigade, but, due to the shortage of cruisers, they had to be equipped with M3 Stuart light tanks. The 22nd was thus able to participate in Operation Crusader in November 1941.

## ■ OPERATION CRUSADER

Operation Crusader (18 November - 30 December 1941) was a military operation of the Western Desert Campaign during World War II conducted by the British Eighth Army (with Commonwealth, Indian and Allied contingents) against Axis (German and Italian) forces in North Africa, under the command of General Erwin Rommel. The operation aimed to bypass the Axis defences on the Egyptian-Libyan border, defeat the Axis armoured forces near Tobruch, lift the siege of Tobruch and recapture Cyrenaica. On 18 November 1941, the Eighth Army began a surprise attack. From 18 to 22 November, the dispersal of the British armoured units led to the loss of 530 tanks, inflicting Axis losses of about 100 tanks. On 23 November, the 5th South African Brigade was destroyed at Sidi Rezegh, causing numerous German tank losses. On 24 November, Rommel ordered a 'barbed wire assault', causing chaos in the British rear but allowing the British armoured forces to recover. On 27 November, the New Zealanders reached the Tobruch garrison, ending the siege.

The lack of supplies forced Rommel to reduce his lines of communication and on 7 December 1941 the Axis forces retreated to the Gazala position, then began a retreat to El Agheila on 15 December. The 2nd South African Division captured Bardia on 2 January 1942, Sollum on 12 January and the fortified position of Halfaya on 17 January, taking some 13,800 prisoners. On 21 January 1942, Rommel surprised the Eighth Army and pushed it back to Gazala, where both sides regrouped. The Battle of Gazala began at the end of May 1942.

In Operation Crusader, the two British corps were arranged so that they could not support each other. It was expected that, being outnumbered by the German and Italian forces in tanks, the fighting would favour the British. However, Rommel avoided committing his tanks en masse against the British, instead taking advantage of a large number of German anti-tank guns, which, operating offensively with tanks and infantry, proved effective. The Germans were mainly equipped with the PaK 38, a 50 mm long-barrelled gun with a range of 910 metres. This superiority in the quality and tactical arrangement of anti-tank guns was to be a characteristic of the Afrika Corps during the 'Desert War'. The Crusader's 2-pounder (40 mm) gun was as effective as the 50 mm short-barrelled gun of the Panzer III, although it was surpassed by the 75 mm short-barrelled gun of the Panzer IV.

## ■ OPERATION BERTRAM

In the context of British 'deception operations', the Crusaders could be equipped with the 'Sunshade', a metal structure with a canvas cover that camouflaged the tank as a truck in the eyes of German aerial reconnaissance. Dummy tanks were also used.

Later in the campaign, shipping improved and Nuffield sent a team of engineers to Egypt; crew teams became more adept at preventing problems, but the Crusader's reputation failed to recover.

After Montgomery took command, the imbalance between British and German armoured units was corrected through better control and the introduction of more US-supplied Grant and Sherman tanks. The Crusader was replaced in the front line of battle and employed in 'light squadrons' to attempt to outflank the enemy when they were confronted by heavier units. The 9th Australian Infantry Division operated Crusaders for reconnaissance and liaison.

## A15 CRUSADER MK. II CS (CLOSE-SUPPORT)

▲ A15 Crusader MK. II CS (3-inch 76 mm howitzer).

# CRUSADER MK. II, EL ALAMEIN, OCTOBER 1942

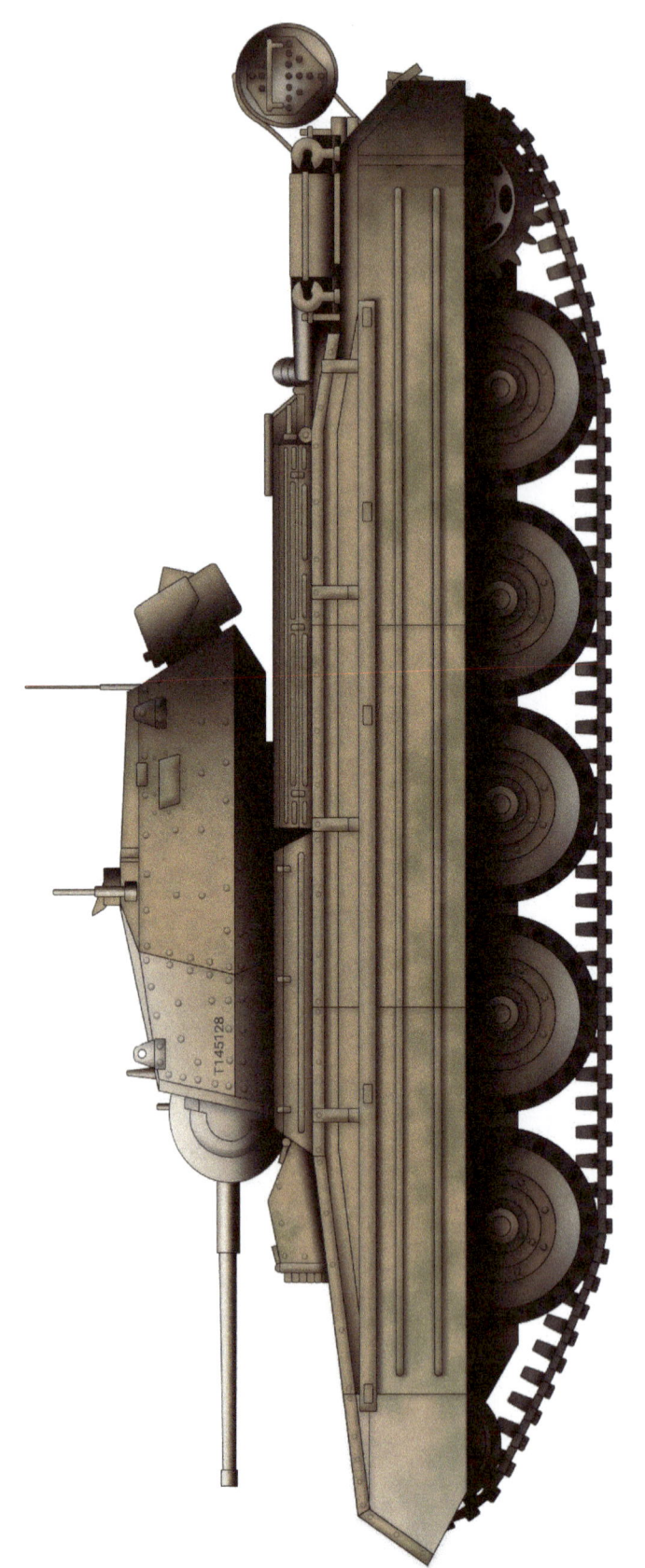

▲ Crusader Mk. II, Reconnaissance Cavalry Regiment 9th Australian Division, El Alamein, October 1942.

## IN TUNISIA

The British 1st Army landed as part of the Allied operations in Tunisia; some of its units employed Crusaders and these went into action from 24 November. These were not just Crusader regiments, but a mixture of Crusader and Valentine tanks; within each squadron, two sections were equipped with Crusader IIIs, and there were also Crusader II CSs assigned to Squadron Headquarters. These units of the 26th Armoured Brigade were used as an independent armoured column, 'Blade Force', with the 78th Infantry Division. The Blade Force operations took place in terrain different from the desert of previous campaigns, and the fighting took place with a reduced number of vehicles. These actions foreshadowed what would later be seen in Europe.

During the campaign in Tunisia, the 1st Army switched to Sherman tanks, but the Crusaders remained in use with the 8th Army for a longer period. The Crusaders' last significant actions were the Battle of the Mareth Line and the Battle of Wadi Akarit. The North African campaign ended shortly afterwards.

▲ The crew of a Crusader tank prepares a meal in the Western Desert, 20 September 1942.

Although the Crusader was faster than any tank it compared with, its potential was limited by a relatively light 2 lb QF gun, thin armour and mechanical problems. A particular tactical limitation was the lack of high-explosive projectiles for the main armament (which existed but were not supplied). The Axis armoured forces developed an extremely effective method of dealing with attacking enemy forces by retreating behind a screen of concealed anti-tank guns. Pursuing tanks could then be engaged by artillery. With the German anti-tank guns out of range of the tanks' machine guns and without high-explosive shells to return fire, the tanks were left with the equally difficult options of retreating under enemy fire or trying to break through the gun barrier.

In addition, the Crusader proved prone to 'catching fire' on impact, a problem attributed to the ignition of projectiles due to hot metal penetrating unprotected compartments. The angled turret bottom created shot traps that deflected the projectiles downwards through the hull roof.

The Crusader proved to be unreliable in the desert, a problem that began as early as transport from the UK to North Africa. Poor preparation and handling caused problems that had to be resolved before they could be assigned to regiments, consuming the spare parts inventory. Once in use, sand caused erosion in the cooling system and the stress of travelling over rough terrain caused oil leaks between the engine block and cylinders. As there were few tank carriers or railways in the desert, the tanks had to travel long distances on their tracks, causing further wear and tear.

These problems, combined with the availability of better tanks such as the Sherman and Cromwell, led first to the redeployment and later the withdrawal from service of the Crusaders.

▲ Crusader Mk. III in Tunisia, 31 December 1942.

▲ Another Crusader tank fallen into German hands of the Africa Korps. Libya-Egypt, 1942.

▲ The British Crusader tank passes a burning German Pzkw Mk IV tank during Operation Crusader.

▲ Tank Crusader Mk. III, 1 January 1943, North Africa.

▲ Crusader tank of a 24th Lancer squadron of the 11th Armoured Division filmed at high speed during an exercise in Sussex on 15-16 July 1942.

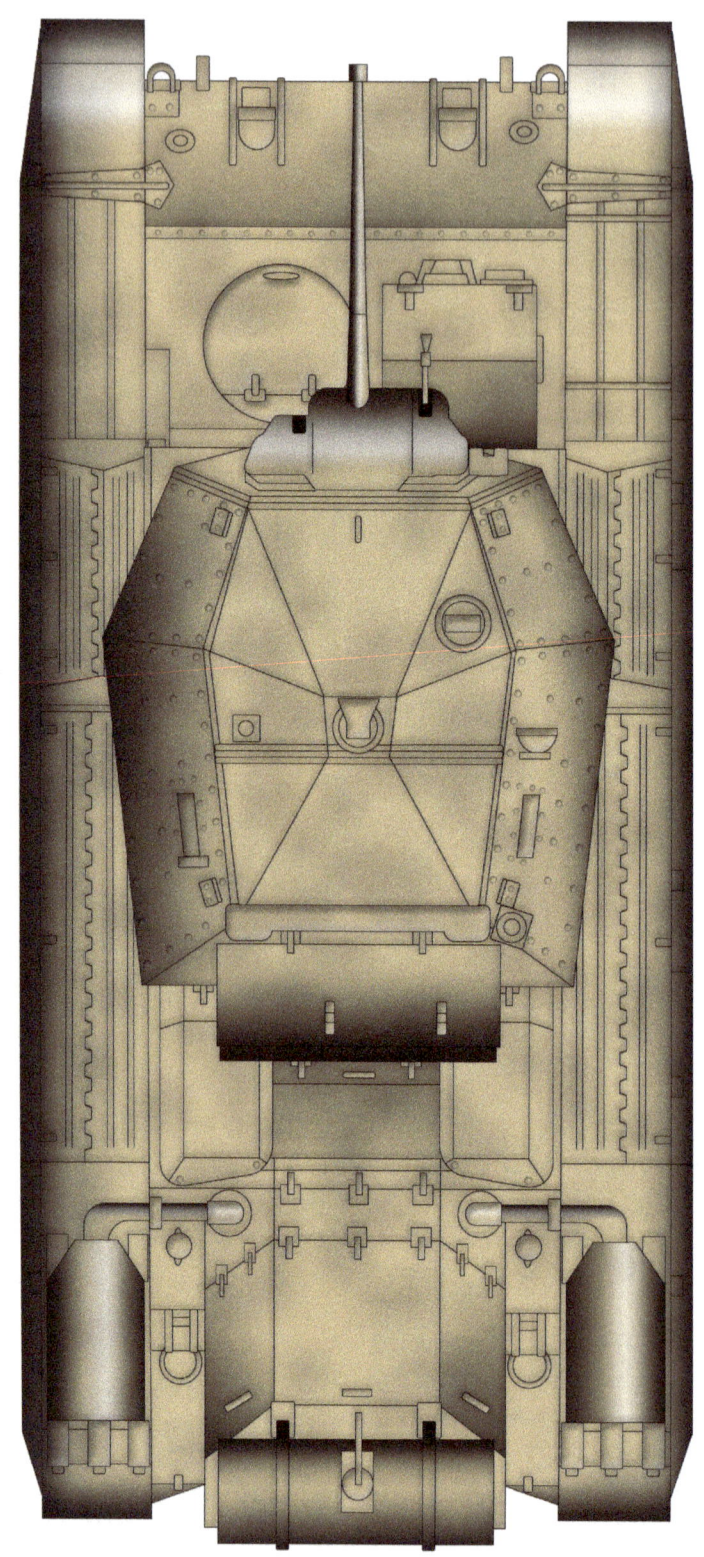

▲ View of the British tank Crusader Mk. II from above.

CRUSADER MK. III

▲ Newly landed Crusader tanks are taken from the docks of the occupied port of Tripoli to the port workshops, formerly of the Royal Army Electrical and Mechanical Engineers, 15 March 1943.

▼ Czech Crusader III on parade, England, 1943, belonging to the Czech Independent Armoured Brigade.

▲ Crusader Mk. III with 6pdr Mk 5 L 50 gun takes part in the parade of the Independent Czech Armour Brigade in Harwich, England, spring '43.

▼ A Mk. VI Crusader III A15 without side wings.

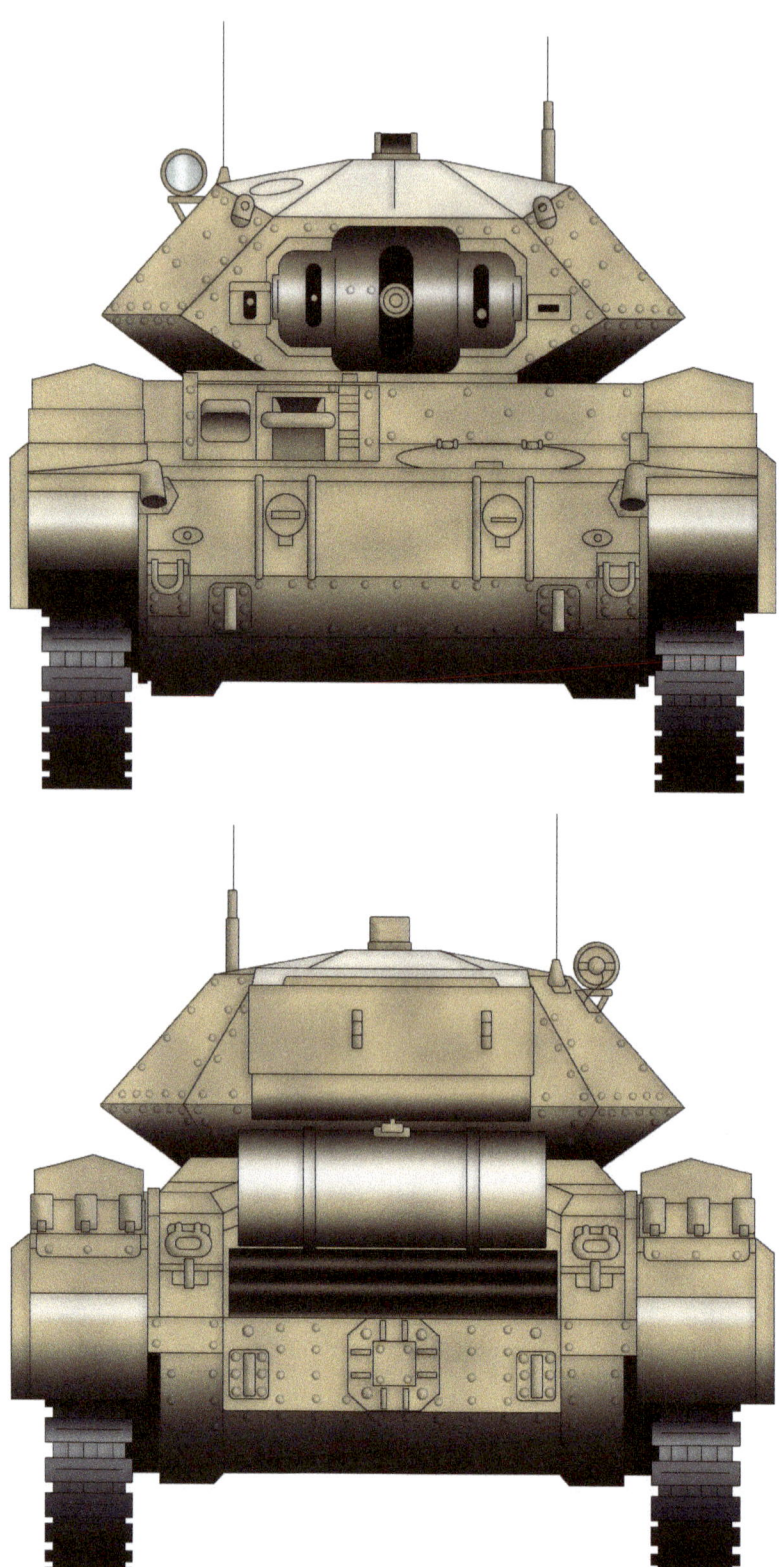

▲ View of the Crusader Mk. II from the front and back.

CRUSADER MK. III

# CRUSADER MK. III

# CAMOUFLAGE AND DISTINCTIVE SIGNS

The background colours and camouflage tints of British military vehicles (AFVs) during the Second World War were determined by a series of Army Council (ACI) instructions and poured onto military training pamphlets (MTP), with specific general orders (GO) used in the Middle East. The paint was supplied to the units pre-mixed (PFU prepared for use) corresponding to two British standards: BS381C from 1930 and BS987C from 1942-45.

Contemporary photographs and the testimonies of veterans confirm that, with a few slight variations, these orders were mostly strictly adhered to but, as far as the models used were concerned, there were sometimes slight variations. The regulations, for example, provided for immediate application of the new regulations, however, even to exhaust old paint stocks, the old colour was often opted for

This led to the appearance of very curious colourings at times, often with interesting results involving all four basic colours.

## ■ EUROPEAN AND METROPOLITAN THEATRE COLOURS

Immediately after the end of the First World War, vehicles and AFVs continued to be painted as in 1914-18. In the 1920s, various colours were used, mainly the discounted browns, greens and greys. Officially these were called 'service colours', which are difficult to establish today.

However, in the early 1930s these colours were mainly a light khaki or greenish ochre.

The interiors of the vehicles were always a silver colour from the 1930s until around mid-1940, when glossy white was used for all. Soon after, and at least until early 1939, the service colour became a glossy *deep bronze green*.

In the first two years of the war, and more precisely from 1939 to 1941, horizontal/diagonal patterns of two different types of green were practised on military vehicles. The usual basic colour was khaki green with a dark green breaker called No. 4, or rarely light green No. 5, and alternatively *green* 3.

From the mid-1940s *dark tarmac* began to replace the two greens No. 4 and 5. Apparently, this choice was motivated by the need to preserve stocks of chromium oxide, an element needed to produce strong colours and a certain degree of infrared immunity. Between 1941 and 1942, the British standard camouflage colours (SCC) of the second British standard came into use until, once the old paint stocks were exhausted, both the greens and the *dark tarmac replaced them*.

However, shortages in supply and availability, caused by the scarcity of green pigment, caused the basic colour to be changed in many cases to brown, which in turn was darkened by a dark brown or alternatively black.

In the 1942-44 period, the diagrams introduced a new two-tone pattern using browns as per the regulations. The most common camouflage versions at the time were the *'foliage'* and/or *'dapple'* pattern.

In June 1943, the 1° Canadian Corps was instructed to repaint all vehicles in the basic *light stone* or *Portland stone* colour, with various areas of disturbance at the bottom of the body and cabin in black.

This was before deployment to North Africa to take part in Operation Husky in July 1943. The repainting included the addition of clear roundels on the roof to help the RAF recognise friendly vehicles.

In 1944-45, there was a switch to the use of *olive drab as the* new base colour, in order to eliminate the need to repaint US-supplied vehicles. From August 1944, therefore, except on vehicles already painted under the old regulations, *olive drab* became the formal base colour.

During the Italian campaign of 1943, many vehicles used the above-mentioned schemes, but others were painted according to the African-Middle Eastern scheme that used a base colour of *'light mud'* with bold black or dark olive green patterns.

Many of these vehicles were then repainted and, eventually, most of the British vehicle fleet was standardised with the basic *olive drab* coating.

## MIDDLE EASTERN AND AFRICAN THEATRE COLOURS

In July 1939, the regulations for this strategic sector specified a basic tone called *middle stone* with variations of *'dark sand'*. The tanks of the 6th RTC A9 began to use the *stone* hue and in May 1940 added dark sand patches. This scheme became common in Egypt in the summer of 1940. In 1940-41 the vehicles were painted in three tones of *light stone* or *Portland stone* as a base colour with diagonal stripes and additions of *silver grey* and *slate* or *green* 3 used in different variations. A scheme used in Sudan included light *stone* or *Portland stone* with light brown-purple instead of silver grey, and *light stone* No. 61 instead of slate for the same model.

The two-tone pattern based on 'Caunter' and used in Greece in April and May 1941 was obtained by using *light stone* or slate or some other unknown colour. Light violet-brown, in short, was used exclusively in Sudan. In December 1941 the use of the two *stone* colours was still imposed, but only a possible third colour was added for camouflage. At first it appeared that slate-coloured camouflage was chosen, but later more and more vehicles with green or silver-grey camouflage or even brown were noticed. Various departments and brigades strove to choose a camouflage that would distinguish them from each other. This continued until October 1942, when a Camcolor range of water-based colours was developed for all camouflage purposes.

From October 1942 a new counterorder: all previous designs were cancelled to be replaced by new standardised designs for certain AFV types and vehicle classes.

The new colours that appeared on the horizon were a basic tone of *desert pink* with a disruptive pattern in *dark olive green*. Black, very dark brown and dark slate were the alternative variables.

These new patterns began to appear on Shermans, Grants, Valentines, Crusaders, and Stuarts; while Churchill tanks, painted in the UK with *light stone*, featured a red-brown pattern in the Crusader motif. Since *desert pink* was a new colour, *light stone* continued to be used on existing vehicles. *Desert pink* was then used alone as a single tone on vehicles without tactical value. From April 1943, the regulation was again cancelled and new models issued with new colours for use in Tunisia, Sicily, Italy and throughout the Middle East. The basic tone became *'light mud'* with black or other in bold patterns used for camouflage. Finally, in 1944, European colours and patterns also predominated in Middle Eastern vehicles.

## EASTERN COLOURS

Until 1943, the vehicles appear to have conformed to UK standards. There are colour pictures of military vehicles in Singapore in *khaki green* and *dark tarmac*. In early 1943, *jungle green* was introduced to be used as the only general colour. But in 1944, *dark drab* also appeared. In 1944 there was a range of colours for camouflage purposes issued by SEAC in Ceylon (now Sri Lanka), but there is no evidence that any of these were intended as a disruptive colour. From 1943 to 1945 there was only one general base colour.

## CRUSADER MK. III, TUNISIA 1943

▲ Crusader Mk. III, 1st Armoured Division, Tunisia, spring 1943.

▲▼ Mark VI A15 Crusader III British series tank t126272 built by Nuffield Mechanisations, preserved at Bovington Tank Museum, Dorset, March 1998. By Hugh Llewelyn Licences CC-2.

# CRUSADER MK. III, GREAT BRITAIN 1943

▲ Crusader Mk. III, 2nd Armoured Regiment, 1st Armoured Division, Great Britain 1943.

## AA CRUSADER MK. III

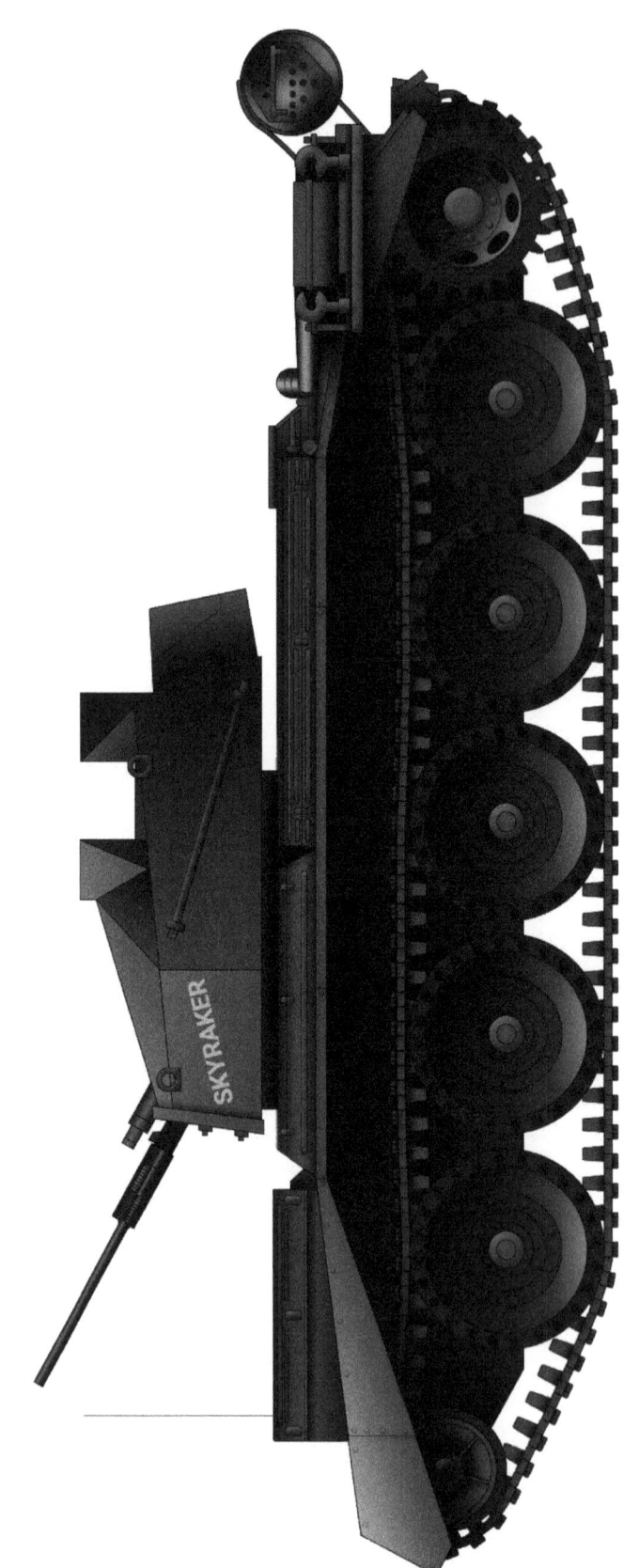

▲ Crusader armed with two 20 mm Oerlikon anti-aircraft guns and a single .303 (7.7 mm) Vickers GO machine gun.

# VERSIONS OF THE VEHICLE

The Crusader tank, despite its limitations, represents a significant chapter in the history of British armoured vehicles during the Second World War. As already mentioned, the Crusader was distinguished by its speed, which made it superior to most enemy tanks of the time. This tank not only had armament suitable for its period, but was also adapted to perform specialised roles as an anti-aircraft vehicle and artillery tractor. Variants of the Crusader, developed during the course of the conflict, reflected the evolution of combat strategies and operational needs in the field:

• **Crusader I (Cruiser Mk. VI):** original production version. The auxiliary turret was often removed in the field, thus eliminating the position of the hull gunner.

  • **Crusader I CS (Cruiser Mk. VI CS):** the 'Close Support' variant mounted a 3-inch (76.2 mm) Ordnance QF howitzer in the turret instead of the 2-pounder gun.

• Crusader II **(Cruiser Mk. VI A): the** Crusader II featured increased armour on the front of the hull and the front of the turret. As in the Mk I model, the auxiliary turret was often removed.

  • **Crusader II CS (Cruiser Mk. VI A CS):** mounted a 3-inch (76.2 mm) Ordnance QF howitzer in the turret instead of the 2-pounder gun.

  • Crusader **II Commando** version: there was a version of the Crusader as a command tank, equipped with a dummy barrel and two No. 19 radios.

  • **Crusader II (gun tractor Mk. I):** was developed to meet the need for a vehicle capable of towing the heavy 76.2 mm QF 17-pounder anti-tank gun. It was a Crusader tank chassis with a simple squared superstructure that replaced that of the combat tank. The 14 mm thick structure protected the driver and the six-man gun crew. The tractor also carried ammunition in the rear and inside the crew area.
  Despite being almost as heavy as the combat tank, the Crusader gun tractor was still capable of high speeds and was officially limited to 27 mph (about 43 km/h). However, this regime was heavy for towed 17-pounders. They were used in north-west Europe from the Normandy landings of 1944 until the end of the war in 1945.
  One of the units that used this vehicle was the 86th Anti-tank Regiment, Royal Artillery, part of XII Corps. In the 86th Regiment, the Crusader gun tractor replaced the previous Morris C8 gun tractors in two of the four batteries. Veterans of the unit reported that the Crusader was popular with the crews and was often driven by former Armoured Corps drivers, assigned to the Royal Artillery for their driving experience. Some veterans claimed to have removed the speed limiters normally found on tanks and claimed that an empty Crusader could reach speeds of up to 55 mph (about 89 km/h). They also claimed to be able to overtake Military Police motorbikes, which were limited during the war to a speed of 50 mph (about 80 km/h) due to low-quality petrol. Some vehicles were also used by battery commanders as armoured command and reconnaissance vehicles.

• **Crusader III:** due to delays with the Mark VII Cavalier and the need for cruiser tanks, the Crusader was upgraded with the 57 mm 6-pounder gun, the first British tank to be equipped with this weapon. Design work for a new turret began in March 1941, but Nuffield did not participate until the end of the year, when it adapted the existing turret with a new shell and hatch.

The turret also received an extractor fan to eliminate the fumes generated by the firing of the cannon. The larger footprint of the new cannon limited space in the turret, so the crew was reduced to three people, with the commander also taking over the role of cannon loader, previously performed by the radio operator. The space in the auxiliary turret was dedicated to ammunition storage.

The Crusader III also saw the introduction of the Mk. IV Liberty engine, which solved many of the reliability problems previously experienced. This engine also included the updated water pumps from the Mk. III engine, along with a shaft drive system that replaced the chain system for the cooling fans.

Production began in May 1942 and 144 were completed by July. The Crusader III saw its first deployment, with around 100 participating, in the Second Battle of El Alamein in October 1942.

- **Crusader III OP:** The 'Observation Post' was a tank converted into a mobile armoured observation post for artillery direction. The turret was fixed in place, the gun was removed and a dummy barrel was mounted in its place to give it the outward appearance of a normal tank. With no need for ammunition, the interior was dedicated to radios, with two No. 19 and one No. 18 radio, maps and related equipment. The Royal Artillery could then operate the OP tank on the front line between the fighting units, directing artillery fire in their support.

- **Crusader III (AA Mk. I):** the 6-pounder gun was replaced with a Bofors 40 mm anti-aircraft gun equipped with an automatic magazine and mounted on an open turret. The crew consisted of four people: gun commander, gunner, loader and driver. However, the Crusader III version AA Mk I deployed in north-west Europe from D-Day onwards did not have a turret, but mounted the 40 mm Bofors gun with its standard shield directly above the hull.

▲ Crusader III tanks in Tunisia, 31 December 1942.

- **Crusader III (AA Mk. II and Mk. III)**: Crusader armed with two 20 mm Oerlikon anti-aircraft guns and a single .303 (7.7 mm) Vickers GO machine gun. The turret was small and polygonal, with heavy armour but limited visibility to detect approaching aircraft. The Mk III differed from the Mk II only in the location of the radio, which was moved into the hull to free up space inside the turret.
A variant with three Oerlikon guns was produced in very limited quantities and seems to have been used mainly for training purposes.
Due to Allied air superiority on the battlefields of north-west Europe, none of the anti-aircraft versions saw much combat against aircraft, but some - especially with the 1st Polish Armoured Division - were employed against land targets. The anti-aircraft units, assigned to headquarters squadrons, were disbanded after the Normandy landings.

- **Crusader ARV Mk. I**: armoured recovery vehicle based on the hull of the Crusader without turret. A prototype was built in 1942.

Some 21 tanks survive in various states of preservation, from working machines in museums to wrecks. Eight of these are in various collections in South Africa.
Among the most notable examples is the Crusader III in working condition at the Tank Museum in the United Kingdom. The Musée des Blindés in France holds a Crusader Mk III anti-aircraft version, while the Overloon War Museum in the Netherlands has a gun tractor variant.

▼ Crusader III AA tank with twin 20 mm Oerlikon cannons.

▲ Crusader III anti-aircraft tank with 40 mm Bofors gun, in force at the Armoured Fighting Vehicle School, Gunnery Wing at Lulworth in Dorset.

▼ Crusader, artillery tractor converted into bulldozer.

## CRUSADER MK. III OP

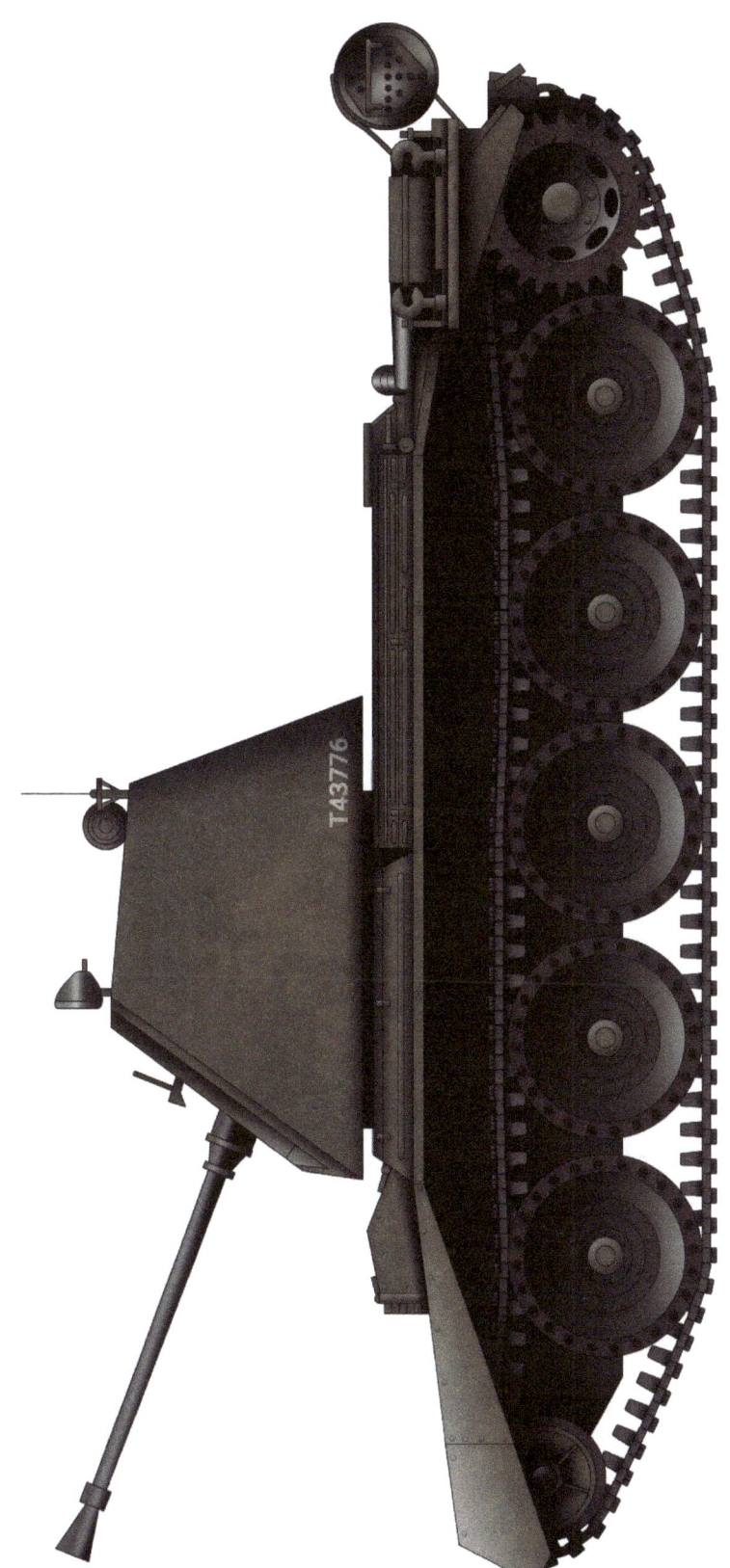

▲ Tank converted into an armoured anti-aircraft vehicle with Bofors 40mm cannon.

| DATA SHEET | |
|---|---|
| | Crusader |
| Length | 5,98 m |
| Width | 2,77 m |
| Height | 2,24 m |
| Date of entry into service/exit | 1941/1945 |
| Weight in combat order | Mk. I: 19.100 kg<br>Mk. II: 19.300 kg<br>Mk. III: 20.100 kg |
| Crew | Mk. I: 5<br>Mk. II: 4/5<br>Mk. III: 3 |
| Engine | Nuffield Mk. I/II/III |
| Maximum speed | 50 km/h |
| Autonomy | Mk. I and II: 322 km<br>Mk. III: 204 km |
| Armour thickness | From 15 to 78 mm |
| Main armament | Mk. I and II: 2 lbs (110/130 rounds)<br>Mk. III: 6 lbs (65 rounds) |
| Production | 5.300 (See note to pag. 19) |

▼ A Crusader tank in its desert truck camouflage 'sunshade', North Africa, 26 October 1942.

## CRUSADER III DESERT CAMOUFLAGE 'SUNSHADE' NORTH AFRICA 1942

▲ Crusader equipped with the 'Sunshade', a metal structure with a canvas cover that camouflaged the tank like a truck in the eyes of German aerial reconnaissance.

BRITISH TANK CRUSADER

▲ Crusader AA tank mounting an Oerlikon triple cannon in a lowered position, 19 July 1944.

▼ Crusader I with the small auxiliary turret clearly visible in place.

## CRUSADER ARV MK. I

▲ Armoured recovery vehicle based on the hull of the Crusader without turret. A prototype was built in 1942.

## CRUSADER II (GUN TRACTOR MK. I)

▲ It was developed to meet the need for a vehicle capable of towing the heavy 76.2 mm QF 17-pounder anti-tank gun.

# CRUSADER III

# BIBLIOGRAPHY

- *John Milsom, John Sandars e Gerald Scarborough,* Classic AFVs No 1 - Crusader, Patrick Stephens Ltd., 1976, ISBN 0-85059-194-5.
- *Thomas L. Jentz,* Tank Combat in North Africa: The Opening Rounds, Operations Sonnenblume, Brevity, Skorpion and Battleaxe, February 1941 - June 1941, Schiffer Publishing Ltd, 1998, ISBN 0-7643-0226-4..
- *Bingham, James (1969).* Crusader: Cruiser Mark VI. AFV Profile, No. 8. Windsor: Profile. OCLC 54349416.
- *Boyd, David (2008).* "Crusader Tank". WWII Equipment. David Boyd. Retrieved 25 June 2024.
- *Carruthers, Bob (2011).* Panzers at War 1939–1942. Wootton Wawen: Coda Books. ISBN 978-1906783884.
- *Chamberlain, Peter; Ellis, Chris (1981) [1969],* British and American Tanks of World War Two, The Complete Illustrated History of British, American, and Commonwealth Tanks 1933–1945, Arco
- *Fletcher, David (1989).* The Great Tank Scandal: British Armour in the Second World War Part 1. London: HMSO. ISBN 978-0-11-290460-1.
- *Fletcher, David (1989a).* Universal Tank: British Armour in the Second World War - Part 2. London: HMSO. ISBN 0-11-290534-X.
- *Fletcher, David (1995).* Crusader and Covenanter Cruiser Tank 1939–1945. New Vanguard 14. Botley, Oxford: Osprey. ISBN 1-85532-512-8.
- *Fogliani, Sigal; Jorge, Ricardo (1997).* Blindados Argentinos, de Uruguay y Paraguay [Argentine, Uruguayan and Paraguayan Armoured Vehicles] (in Spanish). Buenos Aires: Ayer y Hoy Ediciones. ISBN 978-987-95832-7-2.
- *Knight, Peter (2015).* A15 Cruiser Mk. VI Crusader Tank: A Technical History. Black Prince. ISBN 978-1-326-27834-2..
- *Neillands, Robin (1991).* The Desert Rats: 7th Armoured Division, 1940–1945. London: Weidenfeld and Nicolson. ISBN 978-0-297-81191-6.
- *Hill, Alexander (2007).* "British Lend Lease Aid and the Soviet War Effort, June 1941 – June 1942". The Journal of Military History.
- *Orpen, Neil (1971).* War in the Desert. Cape Town: Purnell. ISBN 978-0-360-00151-0.
- *Tymoteusz Pawłowski.* Czołgi brytyjskie w Armii Czerwonej. „Technika Wojskowa Historia". Nr 4 (22), s. 64–77, 2013. ISSN 2080-9743.
- *Sears S.W.,* World War II: Desert War, New Word City, ISBN 978-1-61230-792-3.
- *Stockings C.,* Bardia: Myth, Reality and the Heirs of Anzac, UNSW Press, 2009.
- *Steven Zaloga*: Armored Champion: The Top Tanks of World War II Stackpole Books, ISBN 978-0-8117-1437-2, S. 154, 155
- The Tank Museum: Tank Spotter's Guide. Osprey Publishing, 2011, ISBN 978-1-78096-052-4, S. 33.
- *David Greentree, Johnny Shumate, Alan Gilliland* Crusader Vs M13/40: North Africa 1941–42. Osprey Publishing.

# PUBLISHED TITLES

ALL BOOKS IN THE SERIES ARE PRINTED IN ITALIAN AND ENGLISH

VISIT OUR WEBSITE FOR MORE INFORMATION ON
THE WEAPONS ENCYCLOPAEDIA:
https://soldiershop.com/collane/libri/the-weapons-encyclopaedia/

TWE-028 EN

www.ingramcontent.com/pod-product-compliance
Lightning Source LLC
LaVergne TN
LVHW072120060526
838201LV00068B/4933